TAMMY WAMPLER

Maidens of the Wheel

ORACLE CARDS

Inner Journeys
THROUGH THE Cycles
OF THE Year

Maidens of the Wheel Oracle
Inner Journeys through
the Cycles of the Year

Copyright © 2024 Tammy Wampler

All rights reserved. Other than for personal use, no part of these cards or this book may be reproduced in any way, in whole or part without the written consent of the copyright holder or publisher. These cards are intended for spiritual and emotional guidance only. They are not intended to replace medical assistance or treatment.

Published by Blue Angel Publishing®
80 Glen Tower Drive, Glen Waverley,
Victoria, Australia 3150
E-mail: info@blueangelonline.com
Website: www.blueangelonline.com

Edited by Jeanette Hartnack and Cherise Asmah

Blue Angel is a registered trademark of Blue Angel Gallery Pty. Ltd.

ISBN: 978-1-922573-90-2

Contents

INTRODUCTION 7

The Wheel of the Year 10
A Daily Practice 12
Wheel of the Year Card Spread 13

CARD MESSAGES

1. Alignment — Allanque 18
2. Community — Snow White & Rose Red 20
3. Courage — Berchta 22
4. Power — Antiope 24
5. Sovereignty — Queen Elizabeth I 26
6. The Spiral — Arianrhod 28
7. Still Wind — Kundalini 30
8. Sun — Inanna 32
9. Tree — Hyleoroi 34
10. Appear — Lady of the Lake 36
11. Calling — Nimue 38
12. Dawn — Aurora 40
13. Fertility — Artio 42
14. Foretell — the Oracle 44
15. Inspire — Brigid 46
16. Longing — Nemetona 48
17. Return — Persephone 50
18. East Wind — Dakini 52
19. Allow — Rhiannon 54

20. Create — Pachamama 56
21. Deep — Domnu 58
22. Moon — Selene 60
23. Ocean — Amphitrite 62
24. Patience — Nehalennia 64
25. Ripen — Woods Witch 66
26. Unfold — Hesione 68
27. South Wind — Ninlil 70
28. Acceptance — Lilith 72
29. Balance — Laumė 74
30. Descent — Persephone 76
31. Destroy — the Morrigan 78
32. Disappear — Lady of the Lake 80
33. Dusk — Elen of the Ways 82
34. Focus — Artemis 84
35. Harvest — Mictecacihuatl 86
36. West Wind — the Swan Maiden 88
37. Ice — the Snow Queen 90
38. Rest — Nótt 92
39. Ritual — Wise Woman 94
40. Sacrifice — Iriria 96
41. Star — Sopdet 98
42. Transform — Ragana 101
43. Transmute — Gullveig 103
44. North Wind — the Valkyrie 105
45. Wisdom — Athena 107

ABOUT THE CREATOR 111
BLUE ANGEL PUBLISHING 112

Introduction

THERE IS A LOST TRADITION FULL OF WISDOM, ONE GROUNDED deep in our ancestry. If we trace our lineages back far enough, we might find many of our ancestors belonged to shamanic cultures. Within a shamanic culture, people often worked with a wheel to define themselves in the manifested world. They saw themselves traveling in the path of a wheel through space and time, around the cycle of the seasons, governed by the directions. Because a sense of direction was essential to their survival, these ancestors needed to know the location of the stars, from which direction the wind blew, and where the sun and moon rose and fell. They saw themselves and lived as a part of the natural world.

The Maidens of the Wheel embody this lost tradition. They have had many names—Dakinis in Tibet, Valkyries in Northern Europe, the Morrigan of Celtic lore—and have been known as "sky dancers," "bird women," "swan maidens," "goddesses," "warriors," and "guides to the afterlife." These maidens appear in the Sky Wheel, representing space or the unmanifested. They dance through the wheel just as thoughts dance in our heads. If we are not aware of them, they are chaotic. But if we work with them, they can be inspiring and creative. In essence, they are pure potential, waiting for us to manifest them into the world of form.

Although they are symbolic of thought, the Maidens of the Wheel are living, elemental beings. The Sky Wheel represents the unmanifested or void. But these beings are not all beings of air. They come in all elemental forms and can just as easily be beings of water or earth. Sometimes they take the form of the divine feminine to inspire us as muses, graces, and fates as found throughout mythology. They belong to all cultures and all times, and yet they are beyond culture, beyond time.

The Maidens of the Wheel come to us from the four cardinal directions. Each direction is connected to the four seasons and the elements inherent in them. The messages the maidens bring can connect us more with the natural world by aligning us to the directions and seasons.

There are also Maidens of the Center, for without a central point, there are no directions. These maidens are connected to the sacred teachings of the Tree of Life and to the notion that everything below reflects the above.

In total, there are nine maidens coming from each of the nine directions. The number nine is significant. In ancient priestess orders, such as the Ninefold Sisterhood of the Order of Avalon, nine was a sacred number. Nine was often used to describe the structure of our world or universe: Norse mythology has nine worlds, and in Celtic myth the ninth wave in the ocean is the veil that separates this world from the Otherworld.

Many of us in the modern world have lost touch with the cardinal directions. We do not realize how this keeps us locked out of the rhythms of nature and the Earth Mother. Working with *Maidens of the Wheel Oracle Cards* will help you connect with these elemental beings, reorienting yourself with the primary directions, grounding and healing you in ways beyond your current imagination.

Each card represents a direction, and an idea or symbol connected to the direction and season. Of course, seasons are different depending on what hemisphere you live in. This oracle has been written from the perspective of the Northern Hemisphere but can easily be adjusted to fit the Southern. Use of the oracle is meant to help you realign with the earth cycles. Wherever you are, you are always the center of the wheel. The sun rises in the east and sets in the west. This rising and falling of the sun governs the wheel and governs our cycles. Below is a table that will help you convert the seasons to fit your location.

The Wheel of the Year

DIRECTION: EAST

Imbolc: the start of spring
Northern Hemisphere: first week of February
Southern Hemisphere: first week of August

Spring Equinox: midspring
Northern Hemisphere: around March 20–21
Southern Hemisphere: around September 22–23

DIRECTION: SOUTH

Beltane: the start of summer
Northern Hemisphere: first week of May
Southern Hemisphere: first week of November

Summer Solstice: midsummer
Northern Hemisphere: around June 20–21
Southern Hemisphere: around December 21–22

DIRECTION: WEST

Lughnasadh: the start of autumn
Northern Hemisphere: first week of August
Southern Hemisphere: first week of February

Autumn Equinox: midautumn
Northern Hemisphere: around September 22–23
Southern Hemisphere: around March 20–21

DIRECTION: NORTH

Samhain: the start of winter
Northern Hemisphere: first week of November
Southern Hemisphere: first week of May

Winter Solstice: midwinter
Northern Hemisphere: around December 21–22
Southern Hemisphere: around June 21–22

A Daily Practice

Begin each day by asking yourself questions like, "What energies am I to work with today?" Or "Who wants to help me today?" You can also ask more specific questions about your current situation like, "What do I need to focus on to attract a new relationship?"

Draw one card, or as many as you feel you need to. After you draw each card, face the direction of the card to welcome the energies of that direction. If it is a Center card, feel yourself rooted where you currently are. Think about what that direction is trying to tell you today. Notice what comes to you from those directions as you go about your day. Do you see birds flying from the North? Is there a warm breeze from the South? Is there a storm brewing in the West? Perhaps you woke early and saw an awe-inspiring sunrise in the East. Check in on your emotions and gut feelings to see what messages the Center has for you.

These cards can also give you an idea of what phase you might currently be in. Just like with all of nature, we constantly go through the cycles of birth, ripening, maturity, and death. Where are you on the wheel? The maidens will help you know.

You are part of nature. It has always been and will always be so. You are never alone on this journey around the wheel. There is help for each of us coming from every direction. May these cards spark within you a renewed sense of connection to your most natural state, giving you healing, clarity, and a boundless sense of peace.

Wheel of the Year Card Spread

Once a year you can do this card spread to learn which maidens are working with you and what area of your life needs attention during each season of the year.

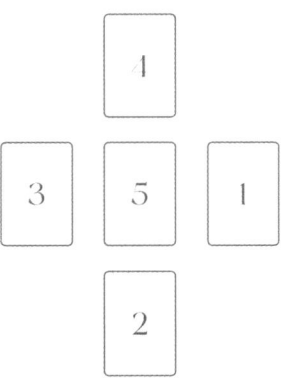

Draw five cards and lay them in a circle to reflect the Wheel of the Year. Position the first card in the East position, and then the South, West, and North. Lastly, place a card in the Center position.

The first card you draw will be the maiden who will be there to guide you during the spring months. The meaning of the card will be what you will be working on during the spring.

The card for the South position will represent your summer, the card for the West your autumn, and the card for the North your winter. The last card drawn will be your Center. This card represents the maiden who will guide you throughout the year. She helps to center you when you are feeling lost or disconnected from your purpose.

    Though this is a powerful card spread to work with once a year, you can also use it at any time to look at specific issues. If you use it to get a deeper understanding of the influences and blocks that might be holding you back, the East position will then become the past issue, the South what is directly affecting you now, the West what is to come, and the North the final result. The Center card will represent what is needed the most at each stage of the issue.

Card
Messages

1. Alignment – Allanque

1. Alignment – Allanque

THE CENTER IS WHERE WE FEEL THE most grounded and attuned with the world around us. From the Center, we can look out in any direction and know where to focus to obtain the wisdom we seek. When we fall out of alignment, we have trouble finding our center. Being in alignment happens when all our bodies—physical, mental, and spiritual—are working together for the same purpose. We become aligned by staying present in each moment, in tune with our purpose, and in sync with the flow of love all around us.

Being out of alignment is akin to being in total darkness. We stumble around and lose our way easily. Many ancient tribal people looked to the stars for their bearings on the earth. Many temples and sacred places were built to mirror the stars and their positioning in the sky to bring order to the earth as it was in the heavens.

Allanque, the North American Leni Lenape People's personification of the stars, offered her light to those who were in darkness and could not see. If you have been bumbling through your life of late, you may be misaligned with your purpose. It is time to step into the Center and call on Allanque.

Allanque's serpent may be interpreted as the spiritual force that runs through her. Above her head is an eagle, representing her higher purpose. The stars are gathering around her, bringing her into alignment. Close your eyes and feel a serpent-like light energy rising from the earth, twisting, and coiling up your spine and around your third eye. Imagine an eagle spreading his wings right above your head. You are in darkness, but as the eagle spreads his wings, stars appear and move into a formation around you. You are now moving into alignment and can see clearly where you are to direct your love in this world. Thank Allanque for showing you the way, and stay a bit longer here, grounded in your center.

2. Community – Snow White & Rose Red

2. Community – Snow White & Rose Red

MANY SIMPLE-SOUNDING FAERIE tales from around the world are encoded with symbolism that speaks of the soul's journey. Snow White and Rose Red is one such story, and it holds a lot of symbolism of the wheel. Snow White and Rose Red are Maidens of the Center. The Center is the place that grounds us and makes us feel safe and connected. The two inseparable sisters befriend a bear who later turns out to be a cursed prince. The sisters accept the bear for what he is and invite him into their community. As they are unafraid of his differences and accepting of him, great love and protection is returned to them.

For many of us, feelings of loneliness can become overwhelming, blocking us from the creative lives we seek. We long for community, but many of us are isolated, away from strong community ties. Relationships give us roots. They ground us and make us feel a part of something bigger. We need them to feel centered and safe.

Drawing this card shows you have a desire for community. This could be a community of like-minded folks surrounding a new interest you might have, or it could be a desire for a love relationship, or family. You could also be longing for closer friendships than you currently have. Snow White and Rose Red thought they needed no one else than each other, but soon found out they needed more when they met the bear. Bears are animals who carry the medicine of introspection. For a moment, meditate on what kind of community, new relationship, or strengthened friendship would be helpful for you at this time.

Center yourself by taking deep, strong, belly breaths. Envision Snow White, Rose Red, and the bear prince sitting around you in a circle. They are laughing and are filled with joy to be sitting in community with you at this moment. You may be having a hard time seeing how you can expand your community. You must be willing to accept others who may not be like you. Relationships can come in many strange and wonderful packages. Snow White and Rose Red teach us to keep an open mind and an open heart when searching for new relationships. Ask for their guidance. Most likely they will guide you to try something new, to meet new people, and to be willing and open to new possibilities.

3. Courage – Berchta

3. Courage – Berchta

WHEN WE ARE THROWN OFF OUR center, we often feel some level of fear. Anxiety, depression, and even annoyance are all different manifestations of fear. Being out of balance can throw us and everything in our lives into chaos. When we have lost our center, it is hard to make decisions or to see the next steps we need to take in our lives.

When we are in the deepest state of unbalance, the guidance around us is the strongest. Signs from the air, the earth, the water, are flooding in, but we usually cannot see them. Unbalance can make us feel like victims, that nothing is going our way, and we do not understand why. The more victimized and unlucky we feel, the more we tend to cut out guidance. It is a cycle that feels hard to break. It takes courage to step outside of the victim cycle. Yet all you need to regain that courage is to find your center.

You are being asked to discover your courage today, even if it seems daunting. Start by being quiet for a moment. Breathe deep. See yourself as the center of the Universe. Since the Universe is infinite, you are always the center from your viewpoint. Ground yourself in this center, knowing you are supported by the whole of the Universe. You are the center star at this moment and at all moments. Life emanates from you and feeds the Universe, and in turn the Universe feeds and cares for you.

See the messengers all around you supporting you and helping you find your courage. The Maiden of Courage is the Germanic goddess, Berchta. In her ancient form she was a protector and known as the "guardian of beasts." She sends out her animal friends to connect with you and let you know that you are not alone. You are not unlucky, and there is nothing for you to fear. You are courageous here in your center.

1. Power - Antiope

4. Power – Antiope

THE CENTER IS A PLACE WHERE WE gain balance, sovereignty, courage, and power. It is where we feel the most rooted and grounded. If we step into the Center, and breathe deep, we can often ward off feelings of anxiety and powerlessness that can otherwise overwhelm us. At the heart of our feelings of powerlessness is a feeling of victimhood. To regain our power, we must create a new story for ourselves.

In Greek mythology, Antiope is a fierce Amazonian warrior, a daughter of Aries, and sister to Queen Hippolyta. Hercules' ninth labor was to steal the girdle of Hippolyta. Theseus joined Hercules in this quest and decided to kidnap Antiope for himself. From this point her story varies, but ends with her death after great tragedy. Antiope's story is of a powerful warrior who becomes a victim, but this is just one myth. In more modern times, DC Comics gave us the story of Wonder Woman with Antiope as her aunt. This story tells of a war general and strong leader of the Amazons. The comic-book Antiope is not a victim. This modern interpretation of Antiope has her empowered and has a stronger resonance. You always have the power to choose your story.

Throughout history, countless stories have been written. However, for thousands of years there have been stories written about women that can be seen to take away their power. Women healers and shamans have been termed witches and harlots; many women warriors and leaders have been erased from history. Stories of women who were most likely powerful—like the Biblical Jezebel, the faerie queen Melusine, and the Greek Medea—portrayed them as harlots, strange fey creatures, and insane. The feminine within everyone, regardless of gender, hears these stories and can feel victimized. The time has come for all of us to rewrite these stories. We start by rewriting our own.

Do you feel powerless or victimized by life circumstances? Are there times when you don't understand why you can't have more money, more love, more health, or more of anything you desire? When we start comparing ourselves to others, we almost always fall short, and then we begin to weave our stories. The "life is not fair to me" story can go on and on in our minds, and the only way to stop it is to step outside of this old pattern and into a powerful new one. In the old myth of Antiope, her captor, Theseus, represents your thoughts carrying you further and further away from your power. You have the power to stop the story at any time and change it.

Step now into your center. See yourself holding a staff, or a labrys like Antiope. Stand firm and strong, knowing that all the power you require is available to you. You just need to claim it. This new story is yours to write, and no one else gets to steal it from you. You are not a victim. You are a warrior, a leader, and a creator.

5. Sovereignty — Queen Elizabeth I

5. Sovereignty — Queen Elizabeth I

STEPPING INTO OUR CENTER requires us to reclaim our sovereignty. The concept of sovereignty has become popular in spiritual circles, but it is deeply rooted in ancient times. It is especially connected to the Celtic tradition of the sovereign goddess. The Celtic kings not only had to rule over their people but were required to "marry the land." The land was thought of as a goddess, and a chosen queen was the human embodiment of the land. Marrying the queen enabled the king to be symbolically married to, and therefore steward of, the land. The Celts also believed that if the queen was fertile and produced lots of heirs, so too, the land would be fertile.

Queen Elizabeth I, though a real person, is the quintessential archetypal sovereign goddess. She is known as "the Virgin Queen" because she never married. It could be thought today that in the Middle Ages, when Christianity had long taken over the old Celtic ways of the British Isles, the idea of the sovereign goddess had persisted. It was unheard of for a queen to succeed to the throne, even more so to remain unmarried, a sovereign to herself. Because Elizabeth was a powerful ruler in her own right, she understood true sovereignty and therefore has become the Maidens of the Wheel's sovereign goddess.

Each one of us is the human embodiment of the earth. We live life on the surface, but have an inner earth, a deeper reality. How deep do your roots go? Are you concerned with your looks and how you appear to the world, or can you go deep into your inner body and live your life from there?

For thousands of years, patriarchal ideas sought to dominate the earth and the feminine, and the body was seen as a source of sinful desire. Thus, humanity's disconnection from the earth and our bodies is linked. Queen Elizabeth subconsciously brought in a new code of sovereignty. Her higher self encoded us with the idea that we are all sovereign beings who carry power in our bodies. When we think of this power and claim it in our bodies, we cannot be owned, bought, or ruled over by another. We are the land, and we are our own stewards.

It is time for you to step into your center and claim your power. You have been feeling ungrounded and scattered lately. When you feel like this, it is very easy for others to siphon power from you. You hand over your sovereignty when you are not fully centered in your body. Close your eyes and draw in some deep, meditative breaths. See Elizabeth appear before you in her coronation robe and crown. She places the robe on your shoulders, the crown on your head. She hands you the scepter and the orb that represent power and the world. It is also your body over which you are now sovereign.

6. The Spiral – Arianrhod

6. The Spiral – Arianrhod

WE ARE CONDITIONED FROM BIRTH to think that everything happens in a linear fashion. This way of thinking throws us out of alignment with nature. There is one dominant pattern all over the universe — the spiral. When we can reconnect with the spiral, we align with our soul's purpose and the rhythm of creation. The Welsh goddess, Arianrhod, is connected to the wheel of the stars seen in the sky as the ever-turning spiral. She teaches us to follow the spiral and not the soul-draining march of past, present, future. Today, you are called to meditate on the spiral.

Sometimes, when life is not going as planned, it is hard for us to see the bigger picture. If we could fly high above and have the eyes of the owl—seeing light in dark places—we would see the design of our lives. The pattern of our lives is not laid out in a straight line, but in a spiral. We often loop back over and over to reconnect with things from our past. Sometimes we feel stuck in a loop, and we don't feel we are making progress. This belief, that progress is something that comes in the future, is what causes us to be stuck as this concept of the future is an illusion.

If you could fly high above not only your life, but also the lives of your ancestors, again, you would see one giant spiral. We loop back, fold in, and touch the lives of our ancestors every day. DNA is a coiled spiral, symbolic of our relationships with our ancestors. We hold all their knowledge within us. We are not caught in a loop, but are a part of this living ancient spiral. All the inspiration you could possibly glean is within you, a part of you. It is coiling and reaching for the sun like an ivy plant growing higher and higher. Step outside of your linear march. Fly high into the stars and look down on this beautiful spiral of which you are an integral part. Know you are of this whole unfolding; your purpose here on this planet is at the center of this beautiful spiral.

7. Still Wind – Kundalini

7. Still Wind – Kundalini

To find our center, we need to quiet our minds and sit in stillness. Humans have used meditative arts for as long as there has been writing. Many people make meditating more complicated than it needs to be. Yet, quieting the mind can feel like a daunting task. Our thoughts often feel like a hundred crows circling our brains, cawing for our attention. The truth is we need to observe our thoughts more than we need to empty our minds. To sit in quiet contemplation is to become one with the still wind within us and to watch the thoughts as they flitter, caw, and squawk. By watching our thoughts, we are more likely to stay detached from them and to not get caught up in the emotions they create.

In tantric traditions, it is believed a latent energy resides at the base of the spine. Ritual, chanting, movement and other forms of meditation are used to release and guide that energy so it rises toward the head and the *ajna*, or third eye chakra. The third eye is where this energy is retained and where it is released. Hindu tradition says all people have a third eye. The two physical eyes see the external world and the third eye sees the inner world. The still wind in the Maidens of the Wheel tradition is the rising energy itself — the Kundalini, as it is known in Tantra. The still wind rises from our center — from the inner earth and into our inner bodies. When we meditate on this energy, and attempt to feel it within our inner bodies, we open a portal to a profound stillness and presence that the ancients termed "enlightenment."

You are being called today to be still and watch your thoughts. You may be currently caught up in a whirlwind of thoughts producing strong reactions in your body. Before you are seized with these emotions, embrace a moment to be still and meditate. Find a quiet place where you can sit and relax. Draw in as many relaxing breaths as you need to feel calm. Any time a wandering thought arises, just acknowledge and watch it. Don't chase after it. When you are ready, connect with your inner body by feeling the rising still wind within you. Draw this energy up into your third eye. Sit for a while, letting this powerful wind of stillness charge your inner being.

Whenever you can, especially when you feel yourself getting carried away with thoughts, try this practice to help you connect with the stillness. Sometimes even a few seconds of stopping and connecting with the still wind within can bring you back to your center and bring about profound peace. The more you practice connecting with this inner wind, the more you will start to see the turmoil in your life begin to subside. Clarity will arise out of the stillness, and the answers you seek will be given to you.

8. Sun Inanna

8. Sun Inanna

EACH OF US HAS A SUN THAT RESIDES in our chests, in our center. This sun is where we draw in love and pour our love out into the world. It resides in our heart chakras. It is our creative center and its energy is feminine. When we align with this center sun, we open a portal into the timeless realm of creation. It anchors us in our being and connects us to the universal flow of life.

The Maiden of the Wheel who represents the sun is the ancient Sumerian goddess, Inanna (parallel to the Mesopotamian/Akkadian goddess, Ishtar). Just like the knowledge of the Wheel Maidens has been hidden, so has the knowledge that Venus is our second sun, our feminine sun. Venus could be said to be the physical representation of the heart chakra, and Inanna, the embodiment of Venus on Earth.

The great myth of Inanna is of her descent into the Underworld. As she descends, she has clothing, or veils, stripped from her slowly until she arrives in the Underworld naked. This myth represents to us the turnover from matriarchal rule to patriarchal rule, where the power of the feminine was stripped until women were left powerless.

There was a slow shift from polytheism to monotheistic religions that worship one masculine sun god. The power of the sun is great; it burns up everything in its wake. The masculine force is the force of action. Without this forceful energy ascending, we would not have evolved into the world of semi-luxury we now inhabit. However, when the sun is left to burn too long, it creates a wasteland. We are on the verge of this now. The feminine sun needs to be reborn, and the land needs the healing waters of the feminine.

Without your inner sun, you are disconnected from your creative self. You are the wasteland, empty, and disconnected from your purpose. You may go about your life performing your duties, but you will be all action and no depth. It is time to find the feminine sun that has been hidden from you. Inanna is here to guide you into the Underworld to find what you have lost. The inner sun is your passion, your creativity, your joy. When you are centered and you feel your heart expanding like it will burst out of your chest, you will know you have found your sun again. Once you find it, you will want to help others to find theirs, too. This is the reawakening of the goddess sun, of Venus on Earth.

9. Tree — Hyleoroi

TREES ARE LONG-LIVED BEINGS. SOME trees living today have been around for hundreds of years. The oldest tree on the planet is about five thousand years old. Can you imagine all the things these trees have witnessed in their lifetimes? Trees know the cycles of the earth, of life, and death better than any of us. Trees sustain not just their own lives but multiple lives around them, providing shade and oxygen for all land-dwelling creatures to breathe. It's no wonder the mythologies of so many cultures hold trees in such great regard. The Tree of Life is a symbol that appears in Norse, Celtic, Tibetan, Middle Eastern, Chinese, and Russian cultures, to name a few. The Celts believed the wisdom held by trees was so important that they formed an alphabet around trees. For them, all knowledge was held within the language of the trees.

In Greek mythology, there is a class of nymphs called the Hyleoroi who are known as the "watchers in the woods." They are tree spirits who remain still and present, and observe the abundant life in the woods. Sometimes, when walking deep in the woods, you may feel eyes on you but not see any sign of animals or people. It is an eerie feeling to some. To others, it feels comforting. The trees watch us and make no judgments. The Hyleoroi are Maidens of the Wheel and are here to teach us how to become more present through the simple act of observing.

Drawing the tree card today is a sign you need a deep, rooted kind of presence. Has your mind been wandering lately? Are you delving too much into your past, your future, your desires, and your needs? Can you stop now and observe the world with no thought? Go outside and find an old tree with ample shade. Sit underneath it and imagine being that tree. Look out at the world through the eyes of the tree. What does the tree see? Doing this for even ten minutes will center you in your body and ground you. If you spend longer with the tree, you can gain some of its wisdom.

You may feel a feeling of excitement or knowingness as you read these words about tree wisdom. This is a sign you are either connecting with past lives as Druids, or the Druid tree wisdom is encoded in your ancestral DNA. Druids, along with priests from other cultures in which the Tree of Life was a dominant spiritual symbol, felt a strong pull to trees. Today, many feel called to rediscover tree wisdom. By drawing this card you are being called to learn more from the trees. Many people have become uprooted and are in need of the grounding that trees teach. As you learn to connect with the trees, you may feel a need to share what you learn. The peace you feel sitting under a tree is a feeling that others will feel in your presence as you learn the wisdom of the trees.

10. Appear — Lady of the Lake

10. Appear — Lady of the Lake

THE SUN RISES IN THE EAST. THE East is related to spring on the Wheel of the Year, and to a time of new life beginning to bud or appear. Many ancient stories tell how the sun rises in the morning from an overnight visit to the Underworld. We find this symbolism of the sun's Underworld visit etched in rock art in the western United States, and in Egypt it is mentioned in the Book of the Dead. The sun made a shamanic journey to the Underworld and brought back the ability to give new life daily. The Underworld, or Otherworld, is the place of the ancestors and gods, and is where we recharge and come back changed or renewed.

There are many tales of maidens haunting lakes, appearing, and then disappearing to unsuspecting humans. Often wearing white and known as "the white lady," these figures are found in ghost stories from many cultures and eras. In the Baltic regions these women are known as Rusalka. In the United States there are legends of women ghosts, like the Lady of Loon Lake in New York. They are sometimes thought to be women who drowned or were murdered by jealous lovers, or faerie women who tempt men to drown themselves. Although harmful energies exists, many of these ladies of lakes are Maidens of the Wheel, guides to the Otherworld.

These fae women appear to us slowly, coming out of the darkness and blending in with their surroundings. They bring messages from the land of our ancestors and the gods. By drawing this card today, you are connecting with an Otherworld guide. What has been hidden is now appearing to you. Messages and synchronicities will likely be all around you, so pay close attention. You have felt ready for change and newness, but have not been sure of what that change is. You have had a vague, gnawing feeling that has felt unclear. The answers will now become evident.

Turn now to the East and ask for the Maiden of the Lake to appear to you. She may come holding a sword, or with an animal familiar on her shoulder. She will bring you a gift from the Otherworld. Accept her gift and give thanks for her kindness. As you are ready to leave your old path behind, the gift that appears to you now will help you create a new path on which to wander. Watch for the synchronicities as magic is all around you.

Lady of the Lake appears in this oracle twice as she brings you messages from two seasons of the wheel.

11. Calling – Nimue

DEEP DOWN, EACH OF US KNOWS what our calling is. It beckons to us in our dreams, and we hear it in the whisper of the East wind. The crickets and frogs sing the song of our calling to us every night in the summer, when our thoughts are lighter and our hearts more open. Every spring, as the world begins to make itself anew, our calling is the easiest to find. At least it should be easy to find; yet for most of us, it is not. We all have gathered around us multitudes of limiting beliefs that block us from hearing and finding our purpose.

The Maiden of the Wheel who guides us in finding our calling is Nimue. A Lady of the Lake in the Arthurian legends, Nimue is described in some stories as an evil enchantress. She was a powerful sorceress who caused the downfall of Merlin, greatest of all sorcerers. The myth of Merlin and Nimue gives us many clues that Merlin trained her as his apprentice and successor. Although the Arthurian legends can be considered myth, they are often believed to be based on actual living people in the pre-Saxon era of the British Isles. If Nimue were a woman living in that time, it is most likely she would have witnessed the power of women being successively diminished;

and yet she had a calling to become a great sorceress after Merlin. To recognize and achieve her soul's purpose, Nimue undoubtedly had to overcome many inner struggles.

Turn now to the East and ask the powerful sorceress Nimue to enter and commune with you. She is often sensed as a calm, blue light floating at the edge of your senses. If you already know quite well what your calling is, ask Nimue for guidance on how best to achieve your goals. If you are like many and unsure of your calling, enable Nimue to open your throat chakra with her blue light.

The channel that runs between our hearts and our inner knowing, or third eye, becomes blocked with all our limiting beliefs, words spoken, and those unspoken. Every time we think or use words against ourselves, it blocks us from our true purpose. *I am not good enough. I am not strong enough. I am not smart enough. I am not rich enough* — these thoughts get stuck in our throats and block us from speaking and finding our truth.

Think of the word "calling." It implies a yell, a word, something spoken. Speaking our truth is how we find our calling. Often, we know our purpose as children, but spend a lot of time denying it or running away from it as adults. It is time now to own your calling. You may still feel like you have no clue what your purpose could be. It's okay to admit that your truth could be just to be alive, to be strange and beautiful, just like everything in nature. Whatever your calling may be, wherever you are on your journey of discovering it, know that you always have been, and always are, enough.

12. Dawn – Aurora

12. Dawn – Aurora

NEW BEGINNINGS AND IDEAS COME to us from the direction of the East where the sun rises. The energies of the dawn belong to the East. Many shamanic cultures, like the Celts, saw the dawn as a magical time in which doors opened to the faerie kingdom, or Otherworld. It is a between time, neither dark nor light, day nor night.

Most of us have only seen but a few precious sunrises in our lifetimes. This is a prime example of how we have distanced ourselves from the natural world. Every dawn is imbued with magic and healing. It is akin to the birth of any being. It is the birth of the day after the long cold night.

In drawing this card, you recognize you have just come through some tough times. You might have struggled a lot on your path to get here, but you are here. The sun has just peeked over the horizon and the veil has lifted. It's time to get up and begin. It is a good time to bring your creations into the light. Right now, they are like a fragile creature you hold in your arms. As you awaken with the light of the dawn, you become stronger, and with your protection these new creations are ready to flourish.

Orient yourself to face the East as much as you can today. As you face East, think about what you are trying to bring into the world right now. Imagine this Maiden of the Dawn, the goddess Aurora, softly whispering to you to awaken. She is warm glow and stillness, and she inspires you with her beauty. As you stretch and shake off the drowsiness of sleep, you are waking up to all the possibilities of your life.

13. Fertility – Artio

13. Fertility – Artio

Artio was a Celtic bear goddess connected to fertility and shamanism. There is evidence of her worship dating back six thousand years in Switzerland. The bear was one of the first animals worshipped by many European shamanic cultures. Bears were sacred animals — they seemed to die during their winter hibernation and be reborn in the spring. Because they used dens in caves, bears were thought to have a supernatural connection to the gods and ancestors in the Underworld. This association of bears with spring and their ability to live beneath the earth was a sign to the ancients that they enhanced fertility in nature.

Artio was thought to take on the form of a she-bear at times. She protected the wild bears of the Alpine regions of Central Europe. She was a fierce goddess and a shamanic journeyer who traveled to the Underworld to bring fertility back to the land. It is deep underground and deep within the womb that fertility resides. All of life springs from these dark places. A woman's cycle lasts for roughly thirty days, but for only two to four of those days she is fertile. Fertility is a concept that has amazed humans since the dawn of our existence. It is miraculous, and yet all of life depends upon it.

You are in the fertile position of the East right now. You have emerged into the light of day after a long hibernation. Your eyes are still adjusting, and your mind may still feel asleep, but you are ready to create. There is a burning fire within you, a drive that can't be ignored. You can get in alignment with this budding fertility by connecting with bear energy. Eat berries and honey lavishly and lie in the sun afterward. We need to be amply nourished to be fertile, so do not skimp on anything that nourishes your body or soul. It is not a time for fasting and deprivation. We cannot create from an empty tank. Call on Artio to protect you during this phase. She sees you aligning with bear energy and will protect you as you begin this new phase of creating.

14. Foretell the Oracle

As the wheel turns to the East, there is a feeling of anticipation in the air. Life will soon sprout and emerge out of the darkness. You can often feel this in the spring, right before the first buds appear. When we can connect with this energy of anticipation, we step into the flow of life. It is here that we can foretell our futures. We may not be able to know everything that will come, but we step into our knowingness just the same.

There are many accounts of people who could foretell the future. They have been known as "oracles," "seers," "psychics," and "prophets." Great stories of miraculous predictions that came true, like those of Nostradamus, have been recorded all over the world. It is hard to discount that some people know the future before it happens. There are times in all our lives when we anticipate what is about to happen. This is not a great miracle as much as it is being in tune with life. The cycles of the earth are always present. When we step into alignment with these cycles, we know what we are about to create before our seeds of thought have been planted.

The great prophets and seers of the past were people

who saw the cycles in nature. There are always signs around us for those who have eyes to see and ears to hear. Slow down now and look for those signs. Nature is speaking to you and trying to hand you gifts. Watch the birds, listen to the bugs, and feel the air around you.

The maiden who comes to sit beside you in the East now is a great oracle. She sees life in all directions, along with past, present, and future. Though you don't need to know everything about your future, you still need to anticipate your next step. Still your mind and feel the inside of your body. Feel the heat and the life within you and how it flows and connects with everything around you. As you sit silently with the oracle, she anticipates your question and foretells your future. Listen to her words before she speaks them. You will soon know.

15. Inspire — Brigid

15. Inspire – Brigid

ALL DRUIDS LEARN THE POETIC stories and epics that have been handed down orally for centuries. The path to becoming a Druid in the Celtic tradition begins with the bardic level, important because poetry is the vehicle of inspiration and is thereby the foundation of the spiritual path. Poetry has a way of switching us from the left, analytical brain to the right, creative brain. The musical language and surreal imagery can help move us into our hearts. It breaks down the barrier between the conscious mind and the unconscious and enables us to enter the Otherworld — the world of the ancestors and archetypes like the Maidens of the Wheel.

The East is where we encounter inspiration. We are inspired to create and to sing poetry as the world begins to wake up and create along with us. Brigid is the Celtic goddess associated with inspiration. She is connected to spring, fertility, and life, and is the patron of poets and creatives of all sorts. Her festival, Imbolc, was held each year when the ewes dropped their milk to feed their newly-born lambs. This was the first sign that spring was returning, and a ray of hope to people who were nearing the end of their winter food rations.

Do you feel you are at the end of your rations? Maybe you have been looking everywhere for inspiration and finding your creative cupboards bare. We go through many cycles of expansion and contraction in life. Often, we find ourselves at the end of a contraction and we feel as if we have no room left for growth. There is always a balance: every contraction will make the way open for an equal expansion.

Brigid has shown herself to you today to guide you to inspiration. Start by absorbing poetry. Don't just read it, immerse yourself in it. Feel the words. Any poet you are drawn to will be perfect for you. Let go of the need to analyze or the need to think too much about the words. Let yourself be sung into the void. All of creation comes out of darkness. Inspiration comes out of nowhere, yet it is everywhere.

16. Longing — Nemetona

16. Longing – Nemetona

WHEN WE ARE LONGING, WE LOOK TO the East. Sometimes we know what we are longing for, and sometimes we do not. Our longing can be for something we can't quite name. It is often wrapped in a belief that we are not bringing our full potential into our current lives. It can bring feelings of guilt, despair, and grief. We can sometimes feel the seeds of possibilities, but are unsure of how to get them to grow or what they will grow into. This yearning for something unknown can be the impetus to act and to create.

Maybe you once had dreams you have now forgotten. When life gets hectic, we put aside dreams for another day, but always that feeling of unfulfillment remains. You are wanting to remember and wishing to fulfill those dreams now. It is time to recognize your longing and honor it.

The answers you seek lie in the East today. The maiden who meets you here is Nemetona, the Celtic goddess of sacred groves. She protects your desires amongst the sacred trees of the grove. Turn now to the East and ask your question: "What is it that I am desiring right now?" If you know exactly what it is, then ask: "How can I bring more focus into obtaining my desires?" Look closely at the signs coming to you from the East today. The wind will carry your wishes, and the birds will sing the songs you have forgotten. It's time to remember. It's time to follow your longing to the East where all things can begin anew. Dreams you set aside long ago can now be picked up again.

17. Return Persephone

17. Return Persephone

IN THE SPRINGTIME, PERSEPHONE journeys back from the Underworld to the surface world, or the manifested world. She is pregnant with new life and wizened from the time she has spent in the dark. Although Persephone has reappeared in the world she knew before, she is not the same person who left in the autumn.

When the wheel turns to the East, there is an emergence of new life — seeds begin to sprout, and flowers begin to bloom. Everything feels like it is being made anew in the spring and there is a feeling of returning to ourselves.

Humans are cyclic beings: always changing, always moving energy. Where do we go when we sleep, when we enter the darkness? When the morning comes, we return to our waking selves, but we sometimes feel changed by the dreams we encountered in our darkness. Every day we go through cycles of birth, death, renewal, growth, and decay. The reawakening is always a homecoming, but sometimes it is bittersweet. Sometimes you are in the middle of a sweet dream that you don't want to end.

Although Persephone of Greek mythology became

a powerful queen in the Underworld, when she enters the surface world, she becomes again the daughter who was taken. Her identities are different in the light and in the dark, and her reappearance is complicated by these differences. Incorporating her new self into her old self requires a delicate balance.

At this moment, you feel the need to return to something you left behind. Maybe you are thinking of people with whom you would like to engage with again. Maybe you are longing to revisit a place you used to live. It could be a hobby like painting, baking, or playing music you haven't had time for in ages. A lot of fear can surround reconnecting with these old dreams or places, as you are much like Persephone in this moment — you are not the same person you were when you left these things behind. Your soul is aligned with the return and this is your current path to the creativity you now desire.

Turn to the East and ask for Queen Persephone's guidance. She is a powerful force and ally. Persephone can eradicate the blocks that keep you from returning. Let her guide you back to the surface world and back to yourself.

Persephone appears twice in this oracle as she brings you messages from two seasons of the wheel.

18. East Wind – Dakini

18. East Wind – Dakini

A Dakini is a tantric deity in Hinduism and Buddhism who can be described as the female embodiment of enlightened energy. Dakinis represent the movement of energy in space and are known as "sky dancers." These dancers are an ancient notion that hints at the practice of the Maidens of the Wheel. We can think of them as energetic thought forms that come to us on the wind — guides to our spiritual growth helping us awaken and raise our consciousness.

The East is the direction of emergence, new beginnings, and things coming into form. As the sun rises in the east, it has been equated with many deities, including the god of Abrahamic religions. In the Book of Exodus in the Bible, the East wind brings a plague of locusts to Egypt as a punishment, and parts the Red Sea, allowing Moses and the Israelites to cross to safety.

Dakinis are associated with the East direction in the Maidens of the Wheel, but are often thought of as destructive and even demonic. They are akin to the Hindu Kali, a force that breaks down our attachments to the material world and is seen as the death of ego. Both Kali and Dakinis are powerful energies to work with. You have to be far along on the spiritual path to even entertain working with a Dakini. The destructive tendencies associated with them are what occur when you are not ready but enlightenment is thrown on you anyway, such as with people who survive horrible circumstances but arrive on the other side with no more attachment to their egos. However, the wisdom of the Dakini does not always have to be learned through suffering. When we work with them consciously, they become a muse and guide on our spiritual paths. They bring us new information we can easily integrate, and grant us ways to emerge painlessly from the shell of our ego prisons.

This card is letting you know you have been working hard on your inner self. Your growth is apparent, and you need to honor your strength and dedication to walking this path. The East wind is blowing in at this moment, and how you interpret it is up to you. You can decide if it is a wrathful, destructive wind (which is maybe what is needed right now), or a gentle, guiding wind. Either way, it is bringing new thought forms that can be instantly downloaded by you if you allow it. It is new, important information you are ready for. You just need to decide if you will accept it or not. As always, the choice is yours. Just know, the East wind has the power to part the turbulent sea and guide you safely to the other shore.

19. Allow – Rhiannon

19. Allow – Rhiannon

THE SOUTH HOLDS THE ENERGIES OF patience and allowing. What does it mean to allow? For some, that word can evoke a feeling of giving up their power. Allowing is a letting go of one kind of power: the power invested in struggling against the flow of life. Summer is the time when our crops grow, and so do our ideas and creations. But we need to allow them to grow. Sometimes we need to step out of our own way to let things happen.

When you draw this card, look at what you are allowing or not allowing in your life right now. Maybe you are blocking something from growing. All around you are messages from nature and spirit helpers, but you may be stuck inside your head and not able to notice. Are you allowing your helpers to assist you? Can you hear them over all the noise in your head?

The Welsh goddess, Rhiannon, comes to you as the Maiden of Allowing. Rhiannon's myth tells how she was once wrongly accused of infanticide and sentenced to carry travelers on her back like a beast of burden. She faced her penitence bravely until she was eventually proven innocent of the crime.

Rhiannon can carry your burdens on her back, if you allow her to.

Turn to the South now. Close your eyes and try to imagine the air from that direction lightly enveloping you. Let it go through you and become a part of you. When you make yourself fluid, you release the blocks that keep you stuck in a holding pattern. You are now allowing nature to heal you.

20. Create — Pachamama

WE BEGIN THE ACT OF CREATION when we plant the seeds in the East. Then in the South, the tough work starts. We till, weed, and water, and wait. We learn the big lessons of creating in the South — working hard with sometimes little progress. Many give up before they ever reach the harvest time in the West. The true lesson of creation, though, is the creative act itself. We can be too focused on our end results, believing that once we finish, we will be happier and more complete. When we are always focused on the future for our coveted happiness, we will never reach it and never find the happy ending we seek.

Pachamama is a goddess of the Indigenous peoples of the Andes. She is the Earth Mother, a fertility and agriculture goddess who holds all creation within her. As the embodiment of the mountains, she is the definition of patience. She creates, and she waits. She is the great goddess of the South.

What are you trying to create right now? Have you planted seeds but do not see much growth? Do you feel like your desires are eluding you or that your efforts are a waste of time? Pachamama has come into your awareness today to help you dive into the deep well of patience she carries within. She has seen many cycles of planting and harvesting, and knows exactly how to teach you to bring your seeds to harvest.

It is time for you to create. It is time for you to work hard; but also, you must be diligent in waiting for your seeds to grow. Turn now to the South. Feel Pachamama's presence as she slowly nears you. Ask her for guidance in creating what you desire. She will be stern in ensuring you understand the lesson of creation before you go any further. The joy is not in the result; it is in the act of creating.

21. Deep Domnu

WHEN THE WHEEL TURNS TO THE South, we have an opportunity to go into the deep. Lots of things are happening beneath the ground, and we can see the evidence of life bursting out everywhere we look. New life is growing and maturing now, and we feel the movement, the ripening. The beauty we see on the surface can be distracting, but we begin to see the deeper meaning when we consider all the processes going on beneath the surface, down deep.

Domnu is an obscure Celtic, Bronze Age goddess who was worshipped in Cornwall, England. She was known as a "goddess of the deep." This deep referred both to the depth of the ocean that surrounded Cornwall, and to the depths of the caves scattered along its coasts. Cornwall is known for its preponderance of tin mines, and so Domnu is also a goddess and protector of miners. Miners have always had a special connection with the deep. Working for hours and hours down below the earth's surface, in the damp and the dark, one starts to lose connection with the surface world. Things that happen above are of little consequence when you are working down in the earth where "danger is double and pleasures are few" (per the ballad, *Dark as a Dungeon*, by Merle Travis).

Many ancient people worked as miners and had an intimate relationship with the inner earth, a connection we have lost today. This physical work inside the earth is symbolic of our own relationship with our inner selves. Do you have an intimate relationship with your inner self? Do you live only on your surface, never taking the steps that lead you deep into your dark places? It is only in these dark, damp, sometimes scary places within us that we can uncover what really drives all that is happening on the surface.

You are being called to do intense inner work at this time. Some call it shadow work, this work of the deep. For your fruits to make it to harvest you need to feed the soil below. If that soil is full of disease, it won't feed you. Turn now to the South and close your eyes. In the darkness, call to Domnu. Though you can't see her, you feel her softly grasp your hand. Let her guide you down deep and show you the wonders below.

22. Moon – Selene

22. Moon – Selene

IN THE SOUTH, WE WAIT FOR OUR seeds to grow and ripen. The South is the place of summer, of long days and warm nights. A lot of time is spent gazing up at the moon in the summer as we spend more time outdoors at night. The moon rules the tides of the ocean, and the tides of emotions within our bodies. When we look up at the moon, its light stimulates our intuition and activates the pineal gland. The moon asks us to slow down and to go deep within. We feel the moon's pull in our blood. It can guide us and help us be patient through the South's wait for the ripening.

The Greek goddess, Selene, was thought of as the personification of the moon. She fell in love with a shepherd boy and asked Zeus to keep him just as he was — young and beautiful forever. Zeus granted her wish, but the shepherd boy was sleeping at that moment, so keeping him just as he was also meant he stayed asleep forever. Selene's love stays asleep no matter how much she shines and tries to wake him.

The moon has the power to wake us all up from deep slumber. We are rarely in touch with our intuition, often looking outside of ourselves for answers. We have forgotten how to go deep within and find our truths. The moon calls to us nightly. We have forgotten her, but she waits patiently for us to remember.

You are being called by the moon to get in touch with your intuition. There are problems you are facing, and you may not trust yourself to know the answers. Your gut knows. Trust your instinct. Go outside and look up at the moon tonight. Imagine her as Selene, gently waiting for you to wake up to her love. She has waited for so long. Greet her, and let her help you remember everything you already know.

23. Ocean Amphitrite

23. Ocean Amphitrite

THE GREEK GODDESS, AMPHITRITE, is the great goddess of the ocean and wife of Poseidon. In many mythologies from around the world, the ocean was the first goddess, the Great Mother, from which all of life sprang. However, the ocean can be a contradiction in many ways — teeming with life yet life-threatening, volatile, or calm, warm, and then cold. It is symbolic of the feminine principle in the world, yielding and watery, representing creativity and emotion. The ocean is a good natural representation of the energies of the South.

You are aligned with the South today. You might feel emotional and volatile, or you could feel calm and creative. Think of yourself as the ocean itself. You are full of life and ever-changing, a force of nature. There is no reason to feel guilt or shame about the big emotions you feel at times. They are like the wind rushing through you and charging the air around you. Instead of apologizing and trying to hide your feelings, let them run their course. Channel all that emotion into something creative. If you can't, let the waves run through you and pass by.

You are called to connect with the energies of the ocean

at this time. Going to the ocean nearest you is the best way to connect. If you cannot do so, find seashells, sand, or scents that remind you of the ocean, or listen to recordings of ocean waves and whale songs. Evoke the feeling of the ocean during meditation, and then turn to the South and ask Amphitrite to commune with you. Amphitrite is a big energy, so be prepared. Drawing this card shows your soul is ready for what she brings to you — intense healing or creative gifts ready to be discovered.

21. Patience – Nehalennia

24. Patience – Nehalennia

Nehalennia is a goddess who comes to us from the Netherlands. She is an obscure goddess, most likely of Germanic origin, thought to have been a patron of sea merchants. Northern European women were often left at home while their husbands went off to sea as raiders or sea merchants. Many of these wives prayed to Nehalennia for the safe passage of their husbands. The sea takes as much as it gives, and many of these husbands never returned home. The ones who did come back sometimes didn't return for many years. The wives of seafarers had to be great practitioners of patience.

Nehalennia is often depicted with a greyhound or large dog at her side. The dog is a symbol of loyalty and patience. Many dogs will wait for as long as required in one place for their owners to return. In the modern world, many of us are running short on patience. Life seems to pass by at warp speed, and there is always an underlying feeling that we need to get lots of things finished, and quickly. Everywhere we go there are lines to wait in and slow cars ahead of us. Waiting for something for years is inconceivable to many people today: they want everything, and they want it now.

This card is showing itself to you because there is a need for patience at this time. Maybe you are waiting for a great love and partner to enter your life, for a new career, or for some form of fulfillment that just doesn't seem to be happening. You are being asked to connect with the slow and patient breezes blowing in off a warm ocean. In your mind's eye, imagine yourself standing on a shore facing South, looking out to sea. Your love (or the thing you are waiting for) is out there somewhere. Gently call to Nehalennia to guide and protect them and bring them into your shore safely. Know that your prayer has been heard. Now all you need is to be patient, and all will unfold.

25. Ripen — Woods Witch

25. Ripen — Woods Witch

IN THE SOUTH, OUR PLANTINGS AND our ideas will eventually ripen. We need to be prepared for this ripening and understand exactly what it is. The maiden that helps us with this is a woods witch. She lives deep in the forest where ripening is almost always happening. All around her, leaves and lives decay and decompose, then grow and ripen, again and again. She understands that almost every plant and seed of the forest can be used for healing or sustenance. The woods witch knows when to take from the forest and when to give back. She watches and waits patiently for the ripening as her life is dependent on this process.

It is often easy for us to set goals for ourselves. This goal-setting is akin to planting seeds. Many of us struggle with the patience to make our goals happen. Because we struggle with patience, we often miss the ripening when it happens. The ripening can come in the form of opportunities handed to us at the right time, or synchronicities that open the way for us when we are ready. We miss the ripening when we feel like a victim and play that old song in our heads: "I have worked so hard for this, and nothing ever works out for me." When this happens, we don't notice the fruit ripening on the tree. By the time we go looking for it, it is already lying on the ground, rotting.

At this moment you have fruit ripening on the tree. You have worked hard for it, and the time of harvest is approaching. However, you still need patience to attain your goals. Turn now to the South and look to the wise woods witch. Ask her to accept you as an apprentice. She will teach you how to watch and wait for the ripening. She will teach you how to attune with the forest: smell the dirt and decomposing leaves, hear the soft sounds of the forest life, and feel the vibration of the trees. The ripening is that vibrating hum, and it is always running through you, ready to create life.

26. Unfold – Hesione

26. Unfold – Hesione

THE SOUTH IS WHERE WE NEED TO listen, wait, and pay attention. Here in the South, we need to regain an understanding of the natural order and the progression of life. We need to let things unfold as they may, even when everything around us makes no sense. Trickster energy is common at this time when we need to be relaxing and letting things just happen. Trickster energy tests us and pushes our boundaries. It can help us get past attachments to rules. Sometimes, this is what is needed to help us relax into the unfolding of the South.

Hesione was an Oceanid, or ocean nymph, and daughter of the Titan, Oceanus, in Greek myth. She married the trickster, Prometheus, known for stealing fire from the gods and giving it to humans. He was always playing tricks on the gods and eventually paid for it — while constrained, an eagle fed on his regenerating liver until Hercules eventually freed him. He is a divine trickster, and although his actions cost him greatly, he helps humanity progress and create civilization.

Hesione is the symbol of us having our lives interrupted by a trickster. She is the divine water, and Prometheus is the hero who brings humans fire. Their life together was a meeting of opposites. Hesione had to develop a deeper understanding of the unfolding of the Universe to see how her husband sacrificed himself for the greater good of humanity.

Has a trickster entered your life without you knowing it? A trickster can be distracting and a smooth talker. They have a way of making you feel like nothing makes sense. Your life is slowly unfolding in the direction it is meant to at this time. Do not be led off your path by a trickster. It is vital you pay close attention to those around you and question their motives if needed. The world is not as crazy as it might seem. You may just be looking through the fuzzy veil a trickster has placed over your eyes. You may also need this trickery to push you beyond a belief system that is holding you back from allowing progression.

Turn now to the South and call Hesione to your side. Hesione is an expert at recognizing tricksters and knows how to handle them. Let her calm your worries and remove the veil. You can then relax and let your life unfold.

27. South Wind — Ninlil

27. South Wind — Ninlil

IN SUMERIAN MYTHOLOGY, THE GOD Enlil, and his wife Ninlil, are a father-mother god. They are wind gods, as their names mean "Lord and Lady Wind." Enlil is associated with the North wind, and Ninlil the South. All the myths of these two portray Enlil pursuing, seducing, and impregnating Ninlil. This is a metaphor for the power of the winds, particularly strong stormy winds that hit in the late summer and early autumn. The South wind is wild and unpredictable, pregnant with power and force. It can be destructive, but it also can be healing, bringing much needed water to dry late-summer crops.

Imagine standing outside in a tropical summer. A storm is rolling in, the electricity in the air is tantalizing and refreshing. Once the storm rolls by, there is a clearing of the air. Things often feel lighter and renewed. Sometimes a storm is what is needed to move stale air and get things going again.

The late summer was referred to as "the dog days" by the ancient Greeks and Romans. At that time of year, they observed Sirius, the dog star, rising at the same time as the sun. For many of us, it does feel like the dogs have the right idea about napping until the heat passes. When a storm blows in, it brings a welcome cool, recharges the air and gets us living again.

The South wind is about emotions, big stormy emotions, emotions we ignore and put off for another day. Drawing this card shows you have emotions you can no longer ignore. They are pursuing you like Enlil chasing Ninlil. It is time to let them catch you. This might mean you need to cry. The water that falls from your eyes is just as healing as the water that falls from the air during a storm. It is a favorable time, and you are safe. Do not fear the storm, let the electricity roll over you and let the water fall. You will be healed just like the dry land, and you will be able to get up and start creating again.

As you face the South, ask Ninlil to come to you on the southern wind. She will wrap her arms around you and protect you as the storm passes. The storm always passes, and behind it there is a rainbow. This is the healing of the South — the beauty that follows some of our hardest moments.

28. Acceptance — Lilith

ON THE WHEEL OF THE YEAR, THE West represents the autumn. It is the time of dying and of transitions. We are heading into the winter, and we need to accept what we know is coming if we are to survive. Acceptance is an act of transition. When we fight transitions, we are rooted in fear. Acceptance happens when we no longer fight the things we know are beyond our control. It is not the same as learned helplessness, which is what happens when we have lived in fear so long that we just give up. Acceptance is not giving away power — it is reclaiming power.

Lilith is a goddess who teaches us acceptance. We know her as the first wife of Adam in the Bible. For some vaguely explained reasons, Adam put her aside for Eve. Adam's act was justified by demonizing Lilith. Lilith became rather obscure until recently, when she was rediscovered and lifted as a symbol for feminine power. This is how acceptance works: our world can suddenly change and feel like it is falling apart. This is the time when we accept life's lessons and learn to survive through them. We need to quietly live through the winters of our lives so that we can emerge empowered on the other side.

Are there things happening in your life you are struggling to accept? Are you afraid of transitions that are coming and wondering whether it is best to fight against them or allow them to unfold? You are a powerful warrior, but now may not be the time to fight. Turn now to the West. Ask Lilith to help you accept transitions with grace.

29. Balance — Laumė

29. Balance — Laumė

AUTUMN BEGINS WITH THE EQUINOX when light and dark enter into a perfect balance. The West is the place on the wheel where we can ease into a slow kind of balance. We are slowing down as we prepare to enter the cold and dark of winter. The dark will soon increase, but for a moment in the West, we can see all the harmony that is ours to harvest.

Laumė is an ancient fae goddess from Lithuania. Sometimes referred to in the plural, Laumės are women of the forest who can take the form of goats and other animals and are often pictured with bird feet. Laumė was once a sky spirit, but was moved by compassion for humans and decided to come down and live among us. She is a goddess of many elements often found around bodies of water, a spirit of air and the forest. She walks in both this world and the Otherworld. Her domain is both the manifested and the unmanifested world.

The time between the autumn equinox and the last harvest is usually thought of as a time when the doors opened to the Otherworld. There are a lot of magical portals that open when there is perfect evenness. Just like Laumė, we can change many aspects of our lives when we understand the law of harmony.

Many of us never understand how out-of-balance our lives are. There is a lack of magic, meaning, purpose, and healing when we are not living harmoniously. When our light and our dark fall into equilibrium, we open new channels of creative power. We do this by making time to honor both our physical and our spiritual bodies.

Have you been feeling exhausted lately? Have you made time for meditation, yoga, prayer, journaling, or any practice that connects you to your spiritual self? Are you too much in this world, never stepping foot in the Otherworld? It is time you bring yourself into a gentle equilibrium. Turn now to the West and call in Laumė. She may come as a goat, playfully nudging you to follow her, as play is another powerful harmonizer. When we are too serious for too long, we can become seriously ill. Let yourself play, dance, and laugh. Find your balance and discover your magic.

30. Descent – Persephone

30. Descent – Persephone

THE WEST IS THE PLACE ON THE wheel of fading light, of transitions, and of the beginning of death. The sun's light fades and the leaves fall from many of the trees. In some parts of the world birds begin to fly south, and acorns gather on the ground. In Greek mythology, the maiden goddess, Persephone, begins her descent into the Underworld at this time. The Underworld is the dark place of death where the ancestors dwell. The Underworld is the darkness that feeds us and where our roots are. We all need to journey to the Underworld to find the wisdom we seek and the nourishment our souls crave.

In the modern, Western world, descending into darkness is often equated with insanity of some sort. We are told we need to ascend into the light, not descend into darkness. In the modern world, we are disconnected from darkness. We have constant light to help us see in the dark: flashlights, streetlamps, porch lights, lamps, and neon brightness. Being out in the dark with no light can be frightening. Our ancient ancestors spent a lot more time in darkness than we do today. They also spent more time in stillness. Wisdom comes from dark and still places, while knowledge comes from the light.

Something is ending for you at this time. You have come to the end of an important cycle in your life's journey. To honor this cycle and this transition, it is time for you to descend into the Underworld. By going down into the darkness and into your roots, you can find the peace and wisdom you need to be present for this death cycle and to understand what is to come next.

Persephone descends into the Underworld as a maiden taken abruptly from what she has known before into a world of darkness and death. She rules there as queen until she returns to the surface world in the spring. We all go through many transitions in this life. Sometimes things are taken from us unexpectedly, and sometimes we are forced to live a different life we feel we didn't choose. We can become a victim of these circumstances, or we can become a queen. The queen is one who descends into the darkness to find her strength, her power, and her wisdom.

Turn now to the West. Ask the maiden, Persephone, to join you on the wheel. Transitions can be scary, but know you are not alone in this journey. Persephone has traveled this road many, many times. She knows the way through the darkness better than any other. Grasp her hand and let her guide you down to the dark and still places where your wisdom and strength lie.

Persephone appears twice in this oracle as she brings you messages from two seasons of the wheel.

31. Destroy – the Morrigan

31. Destroy – the Morrigan

THE MORRIGAN IS AN OLD GODDESS who comes to us from Ireland. Her worship stretches back to around 3000 BCE. Later descriptions of her show a triple goddess, mainly associated with war and death. She, like the Norse Valkyries, accompanies fallen warriors to the afterlife. In ancient times, though, she was just as closely associated with birth as with death. She is a midwife of sorts, guiding souls to and from the afterlife. She is terrible and destructive, but also compassionate and giving. Goddesses who carry both the energies of love and war are a common theme the world over. We modern folk can't quite bridge this dichotomy. Our lack of understanding of death and destruction, or at least deep fear of these things, keeps us from the wisdom inherent in this sacred knowledge.

When the wheel is deep within the energies of the West, it is a time for destroying. We reap our harvest and slaughter our livestock to prepare for the coming winter. We grew these things all spring and summer. We have put our love and care into nurturing them into full-grown creations, but the time always comes for their destruction. The full moons during this time were often known by names such as "blood moon," "hunter's moon," and even "slaughter moon." This was a time when our ancestors would slaughter their livestock or butcher their game deep into the night by the light of the full moon. There is something about the image of the full moon, blood, and death that is triggering. Most of us do not see this kind of massive death. It is akin to war and hard to integrate into our psyches. This is another reason why the cycle of destruction and death that comes with the West is hard for us to process. Many of us are not as used to death as our ancestors were. We don't know what to do with it, and we certainly aren't comfortable making it occur on purpose.

Nothing in this world will last forever. Things are meant to live, die, and be recycled into new forms. You drew this card because deep down you know it is up to you to destroy something right now. It is time to let it die. You have tried your best to nurture it and grow it, but it is no longer growing. You may have heard tales of the Morrigan – she is scary and maybe a bit evil. She takes the form of a crow, and crows, too, are often associated with evil. Cleaners of death are what they are. They transmute death into new life. That is what the Morrigan will help you with now. Do not be afraid. Let her come in. She will clean up and guide you to the other side.

32. Disappear – Lady of the Lake

32. Disappear – Lady of the Lake

THE SUN SETS IN THE WEST. MANY peoples of the past, including the ancient Egyptians, believed the sun would visit the Underworld when it disappeared over the horizon in the evening. The West is related on the wheel to autumn and the time for life to begin to disappear into the Underworld. Many sun-worshipping cultures, like the Egyptians, also believed that the ancestors went off to the West when they passed from this world.

As we stand and watch a sunset, the darkness seems to rise from behind us. In that moment, we can feel the powerful shift from light to darkness. It is a transitional moment related to the edge or between-place energy of the West. As the darkness envelopes us, we can disappear.

All over the world there are tales of lakes haunted by women who disappeared, or by faerie women. We find this a lot in Celtic legends and in particular the lakes in Wales. These lakes in faerie lore are often thought of as gateways to the Otherworld. These ladies of the lake are Maidens of the Wheel and can help guide you on an Otherworld journey.

This card calls you to release the ideas you feel define

you in this moment. You are being asked to dissolve into your surroundings and feel the flow of life around you. It is in the darkness that we often are finally able to see. It's okay to get out of your head and away from technology. It's time to drop down into the Underworld and disappear for a bit. The Underworld can feed and nourish us. It's time to recharge by disappearing. In this disappearing, you can connect with your ancestors and uncover the wisdom they need to share with you.

Turn now and face the West. If it is at the time of sunset, even better. Ask this Maiden of the Lake to teach you the trick of disappearing. In North America, the call of the loon can often be heard at sunset. His cry is haunting, almost otherworldly. If you have never heard a loon, go find a recording and listen. Loons know the sacred act of disappearing and can guide you in this act as well.

Lady of the Lake appears twice in this oracle as she brings you messages from two seasons of the wheel.

33. Dusk – Elen of the Ways

THE DUSK BELONGS TO THE WEST, as it is a time of disappearing. The dusk is another between-time, the twin of Dawn, its opposite on the wheel. Whereas the dawn is a time of new beginnings, the dusk is a time of endings. The darkness rises behind us instead of receding. There is as much magic in the dusk as there is in the dawn, but it is the magic of going within instead of going out. With the dawn, we prepare to go out and do things in the world. With dusk, we go within to find our creative source.

The archetypal Maiden of the Dusk is the ancient Celtic deer goddess, Elen of the Ways. Elen was connected to the paths of the reindeer and ley lines within the earth. She is a protector of all hidden pathways, including the dream pathways. She guides us in the darkness to find the hidden paths.

In drawing this card, you are connecting with the old gods and old magic. The antlered one has come to wake you from your dream of suffering in the manifest world. It is time to walk the shimmering paths that open at dusk. What you see as increasing dark in your life is an opportunity to go deep within and find the magic that lies fallow waiting for you to remember it.

Are you too wrapped up in your troubles? Have you lost something you were not ready to let go of? You may be feeling a great pain or loss right now, but you are not alone, and you have help to show you the way. There is magic in the air in this between-time in your life. Look to the West and to the antlered goddess as she directs you to the path forward that you currently are unable to see. Your path ahead is shining bright and is infinite with possibilities.

34. Focus – Artemis

34. Focus Artemis

THE WEST IS WHERE WE BEGIN TO obtain our goals. It is the direction and time of the harvest. Although it feels like the time of completion, it is the time where the most focus is needed. This is not the same as the focus needed to develop plans or plant seeds. This focus is more akin to discernment, the ability to decide between truth and error, right and wrong. Many things will happen to tempt us away from our plans right before the time of harvest. We need extreme focus and discernment to stay the course and accomplish what we set out to achieve.

Artemis, the Greek goddess of the hunt, is the maiden who now guides you with her intense focus. Artemis is an avid and skilled hunter. Her ability with a bow and arrow is precise and unrivaled. The greatest of hunters know how to let the outside world fade away when they focus on their target, allowing nothing to distract them. The world is full of unnecessary distractions. Misinformation can come from any direction. During distracting times, being a conscious creator can be difficult. If you have been working to create something for a while and just can't seem to make it happen, you may be caught in the energy of the West and need great focus to reach your goal of completion.

Spend time away from technology and avoid other sources of distraction. Instead, face the West and call Artemis to assist you in this moment. She steps out of the forest and walks toward you. As she approaches, she hands you her bow and quiver of arrows. Take the bow and nock an arrow in place. Slowly pull the bow string and shoot the arrow at your target. Feel how smoothly and easily you hit your target when you are focused. Know that any distractions only make it harder and more time-consuming for you to reach your goal. You have come so far, do not be led off your path now. Artemis will help guide you, and the time of harvest will be soon.

35. Harvest – Mictecacihuatl

HARVEST WAS TRADITIONALLY A time of abundance. It was a time to be grateful, and often a lot of time was spent honoring ancestors for their part in bringing about the harvest. There are harvest festivals the world over that are still practiced today, but many have lost their original meaning. The Day of the Dead festival celebrated in Central and South American countries still honor the ancestral dead, but many do not realize it was originally a harvest festival.

The Aztecs celebrated harvest by honoring a great goddess of the Underworld, Mictecacihuatl. She was the harvester of souls. To a farming culture, the act of harvesting is, in a sense, killing. The last great harvest before winter was the beginning of the time of dying, and the goddess of birth and death was honored in her crone—or death—form, at a last harvest festival. The act of taking a life to sustain another is at the heart of all life on earth. We all become the death goddess when we take in the harvest. We complete or kill something at the end of a cycle. One lesson of creation is always to give as much as you receive.

Though we may not farm or hunt for our food anymore,

we still go through the cycles of creation, and these cycles still coincide with the earth cycles of birth and death. If you drew this card today, you are in the West cycle, and it is time to harvest what you have grown. It is time to give thanks to your ancestors for their part in your harvest. As your ancestors blessed your harvest, how can your harvest bless others? Many people have helped you, guided you, and been patient with you, to get you to this point of harvest. How can you return the favor?

Turn now to the West. Invite the great Underworld goddess to your harvest table. Share your harvest with many, and your harvest will be even more fruitful in the future. Know you will always have enough to sustain you through the times of scarcity. There is always plenty, and you are always taken care of.

36. West Wind – the Swan Maiden

36. West Wind the Swan Maiden

THE WEST WIND HAS BEEN described by some cultures as soft and feminine. Some have described it as harsh and destructive. It is the wind that blows the leaves off the deciduous trees in the autumn. In this way, it seems to usher in death and the end cycle that will soon be winter. But the West wind also spreads seeds that will be buried in the earth and bring new life in the spring. The West wind is a complicated wind. Our feelings about it may vary depending on our memories of autumn.

The West wind is represented by the Swan Maiden on the Wheel of Maidens. Swan Maiden stories tell of a fae creature that is half woman and half swan. She becomes a woman when she slips off her swan skin. A human man often sees her and captures her by stealing her swan cloak. The Swan Maiden marries the man, and has his children, but always longs for her life as a swan. She eventually finds her swan skin and returns to the wild, leaving her human family behind.

The animal wife is a common theme in faery tales and symbolizes our human desire to return to the wild. Society often chokes out any wild tendencies we have. We follow the rules and live obediently, but something in the forest, in the air, or in the ocean calls us to return. Maybe, it is really the wind whispering to us, calling us back to our wildness.

The West is the place where the darkness returns, and the darkness calls us to go within. Deep within us all is where our own swan cloak is hidden. It is our key to returning to our wild selves, free from all the societal conditioning that has stifled our creative nature. Can you feel the West wind calling to you now? Spend today trying to find the West wind. Talk to her and let her show you where your cloak is hidden. You are being called to let go of all the rules and obligations you are currently drowning in. Ride the West wind with the Swan Maiden, and let it deliver you into the unknown.

37. Ice the Snow Queen

37. Ice — the Snow Queen

IN MANY COLDER REGIONS, THERE are legends of a snow or ice queen. She's usually a fae-like being who perpetuates winter and the death it brings. The overall perception of ice is that it is destructive and harsh. But ice plays another role in nature; that is, the role of the preserver. For ages, humankind has preserved food with ice. Humans who have died in icy areas have been preserved and have contributed much to our understanding of ancient peoples. When the ice melts, we can find many things we didn't know existed before the ice covered the ground.

Many times, we put things off for later. In a sense, we preserve our dreams, hopes, and goals in ice. We can keep things static and frozen for years. You have encountered the Snow Queen today because it is time to look at what you have frozen or what needs to freeze. Are you distracted by an idea or goal that is for another time? Is now the time to bring an old dream you put off back out into the light of day?

The Snow Queen brings the magical transformative power of ice into your life today. It is one of the most powerful forces on the planet, and you are now ready to work with it.

If you want to pursue something you froze long ago, now is the time to let the ice transform into water and softly reveal your well-preserved dreams. There is no reason to feel guilty that it took you so long to return to these goals. The earth goes through many cycles of freezing and melting, and some ice ages last a long time. The earth knows that some things need to be protected longer than others. Honor your current cycles and do not dwell on past ones.

  If you feel like your life is spinning out of your control, freeze a few things for the time being. Let whatever is not working right now be encased in ice and safeguarded until you have another perspective on it. This is the power the North bestows; it enables you to look deeply at what is most important for your current survival. Face the North and give thanks to the Snow Queen for helping you learn the lesson of ice.

38. Rest – Nótt

38. Rest – Nótt

NÓTT IS THE PERSONIFICATION OF the night in Norse mythology. She is a goddess of darkness, sleep, and dreams. She rides a horse named Hrímfaxi who breathes out the dew that blankets the earth at night. She brings us all dreams and a good night's rest. In this way, Nótt is the goddess of rest. She gives us that feeling that it's okay to lay our sorrows down and rest for a while.

The North is the place of endings that are also beginnings. Between each ending there is a small space for us to rest before we start again. When we are deeply grieved because of an ending or a death, it is vital for us to pause for a moment, relax, and sleep. Often, we try to fight through the pain or stress that accompanies endings. We are told to be strong, go on, keep working, keep producing. The Western world, especially, cheers for us to constantly produce and looks down on us for resting. The North is here to offer a different story.

In the Norse mythological universe there are nine worlds. Each of these nine worlds has a different name for Nótt, or night. In Midgard, our human world, she is known as

"Night." In the land of the giants, she is known as both "the Lightless" and "the Unsorrowing." To the elves she is known as "Sleep's Joy." To the dwarves she is "the Weaver of Dreams." All these descriptions give us a sense of letting go of our sorrows and the blissful joy that comes when we sleep. There are only dreams in sleep. We lose our waking self and become someone new, someone unburdened with the sorrow and pain we might be experiencing when we are awake. The joy of sleep balances our grief.

You need healing right now. It may be healing in your body, your mind, or your heart. You may feel like you lost something important recently. Whether the death of a loved one just occurred, or a part of your old self died, you feel grief stuck in you and it is not moving on. Pause everything and rest. Stop running in a thousand different directions. Stop doing all the things you think you need to do right now. The only thing you need to do is sleep. Your current sleep cycle might be poor. Maybe you can't remember the last time you slept a whole night straight through. You are in need of Nótt's sweet embrace.

If you cannot rest now, try to get better sleep at night. Indulge in warm baths before sleep. Turn off your electronic devices at least an hour before bed. Read a book to relax, and sip chamomile tea. A good night's rest is your main priority at this moment. Before bed tonight, turn to the North and call in Nótt. She will ride in on her black horse — the dew from Hrímfaxi's breath will be a gentle sleep inducer, and Nótt will watch over you as you enter the Unsorrowing. The deep sleep you deserve will be yours, and the stress of the day will be dissolved.

39. Ritual – Wise Woman

39. Ritual – Wise Woman

RITUAL IS A PART OF OUR DAILY LIVES, even if we are not aware of it. We each have small daily rituals, but true ritual involves becoming aware of the cycles in our lives, and then consciously harnessing the power of those cycles. You might feel disconnected from this world if you do not engage in some form of ritualistic spiritual practice.

Even for the non-religious, a certain amount of sacred ritual is observed at the end of the year. Somewhere within us, we all realize that the North seethes with power and is waiting for us to become aware of it. It lies fallow in the cold ground, but continues to hum with the pulse of life that will reawaken in the spring. Ancient people often performed sacred rituals in the middle of winter. These rituals called to the humming in the earth and beckoned it back to life. Later these rituals became festivals and celebrations, often honoring the births of gods. People forgot the original meaning of the festivals, but they still performed the rituals. The North begs us to carry out the rituals and to remember why we perform them.

In the North, the world stops to rest and recover. Everything goes quiet and still at this time. When the wheel turns to the North, we are at an end cycle. Things are dying and we are shedding our skins. To reawaken ourselves from our slumbers we can conduct a ritual of remembrance. That is what you are being called to do now — remember the healing energy of life itself that hums inside of you.

Many women who were labeled witches in the past were simply healers. The rituals they performed were in accordance with the energy that encircles the earth and flows through all of life on and within it. You need healing at this time. The Wheel Maiden who comes from the North is a witch, a healer and a wise woman. In her hat, she carries the herbs that speak to her. They tell her exactly whom to take them to, whom to heal. Close your eyes and picture her now. She hands you a sprig of herbs and teaches you a ritual to perform. Your body and mind are not in balance, but by following her guidance you will find life humming deep within you, awakening and ready to flourish again.

10. Sacrifice – Iriria

40. Sacrifice – Iriria

THE NORTH IS THE PLACE WHERE cycles end and begin again. When the long, dark, cold winter descends upon us, there is a feeling of helplessness and then surrender. We go through many emotions in the winter as we search for the calm feeling of spring. Though before you can create something new, you will have to let something die. This is one of the greatest laws that exists in nature. There is always a give and a take. What will you give up? What will you sacrifice?

The word "sacrifice" may be triggering because it can bring about thoughts of the human offerings that were common in ancient times. Some peoples of the past, such as the Aztec and Norse cultures, saw it as an honor to offer themselves up for a sacrifice for their community. A sacrifice was made for many different reasons. It could have been because crops were dying, to bless a union, or to protect the community from invaders. They often needed to calm a god, or two, and they did it by offering up something precious.

There is something that is no longer working in your life. It is time to recognize you are at the end of a cycle. What can you give up so you can return to a state of calm? Turn now to the North and welcome in Iriria, the Central American, Bribri goddess of the earth and sacrifice. She is a brave warrior, willing to die for her people so they might live on. She can guide you on this journey of sacrifice and make it less frightening. It is a sacred act, an offering. You have been given many gifts in this lifetime, and now it's time to give back. Make your sacrifice and prepare for a new cycle. Once you have let go of what isn't working, new opportunities will come to you. There will be a new sense of balance in your life as you feel a renewed sense of purpose and drive.

41. Star Sopdet

THERE IS DEEP SYMBOLIC MEANING for the North in Sirius, the brightest star in the night sky. Sirius has been revered all over the world stretching back into antiquity, and has been often referred to by different cultures as the "dog star" or the "wolf star." It carries the energy of the wolf or dog in that it is a guide and a teacher. Sirius leads us back to the wisdom of our origins and helps us remember the principle of the ouroboros — the snake devouring its own tail. This symbolizes the never-ending cycle of death and rebirth. Here is the deepest lesson of the North: that death is also a beginning and that our origins are one of the keys to understanding life.

Sopdet is the Egyptian goddess who was venerated as the living embodiment of Sirius. She is a psychopomp character from myth who leads the recently dead to the afterlife. Specifically, Sopdet escorted deceased pharaohs to their afterlife within Sirius. In Sirius, the pharaohs become transmuted into stars. The Egyptians believed Sirius was the most important star in the sky. The pyramids are built in alignment with both Sirius and Orion, but Sirius is the star connected with the life-giving flooding of the Nile that happens each summer. Sirius is also known as the "feminine star."

Many esoteric teachings speak of Sirius as being the sun behind the sun. Sirius is a binary star system, larger and brighter than our solar system's sun. As Venus is the universe's heart chakra in the sky, Sirius is its third eye. Many cultures, such as the Dogon tribe of West Africa, speak of their origins being from Sirius. The Dogon knew that Sirius was a binary star system long before astronomers with telescopes discovered this fact. It is hard to discount the Dogon People's intimate knowledge of this star and the fact that it has been esteemed by mystics in many different parts of the world. Maybe our ancestors came from this star system, or maybe we are made from the star dust of Sirius. Our connection is worth exploring because our origins are important.

Each of us carries around many stories. We define ourselves and everything in the world with these stories; and because of them, we can sometimes create false illusions that cause us drama. Your task today is to discover the origin of your story. To get to the ending, you have to discover the origin. What is causing you suffering right now? Write everything you know about this situation on a piece of paper. After you write all you can think of, ask yourself what is true and what is not. Where did all these beliefs about the situation arise from? Try to find their origin.

Face the North now and ask Sopdet to guide you to Sirius in your mind's eye. Within this star system is where all the wisdom of the ages resides. Picture a beam of white coming from Sirius into your third eye. You are looking for the beginning of your story so you can receive the ending. In doing this, you become the Alpha and the Omega. You are eternal and your illusions fade away. Your only story is that you are starlight.

42. Transform — Ragana

42. Transform – Ragana

RAGANA IS A GODDESS WITH ORIGINS in the Baltic region. In ancient times she was a powerful goddess of healing and transformation. She was a guide into the Otherworld and helped women through and into their power during menopause. Ragana evolved and transformed through the ages, taking many forms, including a shapeshifter, a witch, and a demonic figure who flew through the night as an owl.

Ragana is a great symbol of the energy of the North. The North has the power to transform us all, but we have forgotten this power. When the land lies in hibernation and the air is bitter cold, there is not much we can do. Our survival relies on the ability to transform either ourselves or things around us. The North says, "Transform or be transformed." In the modern world, we do not always learn the lessons of the North because of all the comforts and conveniences we have today. Sometimes in the dead of winter our power goes out and we need to quickly learn the lessons of the North. We have to transform into someone who knows how to survive, not just exist.

What kind of lessons is the North teaching you today? If

all your basic comforts were ripped away from you, what would be left that still mattered to you? The North always wants you to transform, whether you are ready or not. You are in total charge of your transformation, and can shapeshift into any form you desire.

By drawing this card, you are being asked to transform yourself or something in your life. This could be outdated thinking patterns, habits, or old ways of seeing yourself or others who no longer serve you. You can transform yourself into a survivor, a healer, and a guide for others. Turn to the North now and connect with this powerful and vast energy. Ragana appears in her most ancient form to hold your hand and guide you into this next transformation.

13. Transmute – Gullveig

13. Transmute – Gullveig

IN THE NORTH, WE MEET GULLVEIG, a Vanir goddess of the Norse tradition. She was thought of as a powerful witch, a practitioner of magic known as seiðr. She was so powerful that the opposing Æsir gods felt threatened by her. They tried to kill her many times, first by stabbing and later by burning her three times. She survived all of these attempts at her life. Each time she survived death she became stronger than before. She eventually became the most powerful völva or oracle of the land. Part of her name means "gold" since she is changed by the fire, so there is a lot of symbolism for the alchemical act of transmutation in her story.

Transmutation fully changes one thing into another. The difference in transmuting and transforming is that transformations mostly happen on the surface. When we transform ourselves, we may change the way we think certain thoughts or something about our appearance. We may change habits, or ways of thinking, but our essence stays the same. When we transmute, we become something completely different. Spiritually speaking, transformation is the first step to transmutation. In alchemical terms, the dense matter becomes gold, and gold is a symbol for the soul. Gullveig survived death three times. She transmuted fear and matter into power and eternal life.

In the North, transmutation is the end of the death cycle and occurs right before we are reborn. You have experienced many little deaths as you have journeyed through the wheel this year and in your lifetime. Each time we die to one thing, we are reborn to another. We are constantly transmuting energy into something else on some level.

It is time to shed your skin and transmute into a new you. What is called for is bigger than a transformation. You are becoming something greater and more powerful. Don't let fear hold you back here. Think of Gullveig facing spears and fire. Like Gullveig, you may face a trial. You will be put to the fire, but it will give you power instead of taking it away. Turn and face the North. Call to Gullveig as she sees far into the future and knows your destiny ahead. Let her show you the way through the fire.

44. North Wind – the Valkyrie

44. North Wind – the Valkyrie

HAVE YOU EVER BEEN CAUGHT walking against the wind in the winter? It can bring about a moment of complete helplessness as you struggle to move against an icy gale. The North wind is harsh and unforgiving. The wind alone can cause death to anyone caught in it. It teaches us that we cannot control everything. Sometimes we need to accept our struggles instead of fighting against them to have any hope of moving forward.

The North wind is represented by the Norse Valkyrie in the Maidens of the Wheel. The Valkyries were terrifying archetypes of the carrion birds that swoop down after a battle to eat the bodies of the dead. The Valkyries were said to decide who lived and who died in battle and would carry the souls of dead warriors to Valhalla, the Otherworld palace of war heroes. A Valkyrie fed on death, but also ushered in the next phase of life. Like the North wind, she is a powerful elemental force that can't be controlled. She is feared, but respected.

The North wind is blowing in your direction. This is a sign that there are unfavorable conditions in your life right now. Things may feel disrupted and chaotic. Fear could be rising within you, and you may not know why. Surrender to the elements out of your control and respect the lesson that is upon you. It is time to call in the Valkyrie to choose what will die and what will live. Sometimes we need to hand our lives over to chaos and allow the wind to decide where we land. We cannot control everything all the time.

Face the North. Feel the wind rising and blowing toward you. It may be full of ice, snow, cold, and damp. It may howl loudly and send chills up and down your spine. It is scary and frustrating, but mostly it feels alive and powerful. The wind is an ancient being asking for your respect and acknowledgement. Ask what it wants of you at this time. Once you listen and know, you may find your troubles are not as gigantic as they appeared before you encountered the wind. You feel alive and as powerful as the wind, and you know that everything is as it should be.

45. Wisdom — Athena

45. Wisdom — Athena

ATHENA IS THE GREEK GODDESS OF war and wisdom. Ancient Greece was a nation-state whose economy was dependent on war. This made Athena one of the most venerated goddesses to the Greeks. Whereas Aries represented the bloodlust of warriors, Athena signified the intellectual prowess of a great battle leader.

The North is the direction that brings out our wisdom. We have experienced many joys and sorrows by the time we get to the North, or wintertime, in our lives. We have fought many battles. It is time to decide if it is wise to keep battling or to retire our swords and shields. None of us want to be constantly at war in our lives, or to be forced to battle at all. There is wisdom in knowing that most battles are not worth the pain that fighting brings. Sometimes battles are hard to avoid, though, and the wisdom of the North can guide us through these difficult times. Wisdom is needed to temper our emotions and to help us see the path with the least struggle.

Maybe you feel attacked or like you have no other options for moving forward. You may feel you need to rise and fight for something. Maybe it's a social injustice you feel you want to take action against, or maybe you are struggling with an illness. It may be time to stand up for yourself or others, but first meditate on how best to do this. Use strategy and be wise about each step you intend. Athena comes from the North to guide you on your journey at this time.

Turn now to the North and call on Athena. Ask her to give you counsel for the battle you are about to begin. Athena can show you that the battle does not have to be scary. With the correct strategy, any battle can be won. Athena brings you the gift of her shield and helmet to protect you during this time. The shield imparts protection, and the helmet gives you wisdom. Imagine yourself wielding these each time you are faced with your battle, and you will find the strength and wisdom you currently seek.

About the Creator

Tammy Wampler's path to becoming an artist was like the ever-turning spiral. She worked as an archaeologist, a massage and reiki practitioner, and a tarot and past-life reader, before focussing on her art full-time. Tammy draws on her deep understanding of myth and history as well as her intuitive knowledge of symbolism and culture in the creation of oracle decks.

Found in public and private collections and exhibited worldwide, Tammy's artworks concentrate on the figurative and are expressed in oils, acrylics, and soft pastels. Her creations are influenced by Magic Realism, Art Nouveau, and Fantasy and convey a strong sense of emotion through the eyes of her subjects. Tammy's exploration of strength and vulnerability is woven with shamanism, mysticism and myth to portray engaging feminine archetypes.

Tammy lives in the beautiful Bluegrass Region of Kentucky, USA with her husband, two teens, three cats, and a golden retriever.

Discover more of her work at:
www.tammywampler.artweb.com

Blue Angel Publishing

Blue Angel has been illuminating hearts and minds since 1997. Our first major title, *Universal Love Healing Oracle* by Toni Carmine Salerno, is now part of an inspiring catalogue of card sets, books, recordings and more. With thanks to an ever-expanding alliance of writers, artists, editors and designers, Blue Angel has become an industry leader, renowned for crafting beautiful products that bring soulful messages and healing to the world.

      A trusted and established network distributes hundreds of Blue Angel titles across the globe. Many of our products are available in other languages, including French, Spanish, Japanese and Dutch.

OUR HISTORY

Founded by Toni and Martine Salerno, Blue Angel began life in 1997 as a metaphysical bookstore, art gallery and natural healing centre. The name 'Blue Angel' was Martine's idea, inspired by one of Toni's paintings of Archangel Michael, who is also known as 'the blue angel' or 'blue ray'. Blue Angel Publishing is founded on the unwavering dedication of Toni and Martine and their desire to inspire and help others to help themselves. Blue Angel is a dream realised through the belief that we are all greater than we know ourselves to be, and that we can access a treasure of creativity, intuition and wisdom when we look within. We give thanks to the hundreds, if not thousands, of natural therapists, writers, artists, metaphysical stores, counsellors, reiki practitioners, vibrational healers, mentors, teachers, yoga centres, intuitives, tarot and card readers, and everyone else who contributes to the network of light and love that circles our beautiful planet.

OUR VISION

Blue Angel is about embracing life love and creativity and empowering the soul. We believe words and images can bring light, inspire peace, raise hope and spark joy. We aim to illuminate hearts and minds through beauty, art, music and wisdom, and we invite creators, authors, musicians, healers, believers and dreamers everywhere to join us. Together, we can help make the world a better place.

Also available from Blue Angel Publishing®

ORACLE OF THE SACRED HORSE

KATHY PIKE
Artwork by Laurie Prindle

As well as offering honest and supportive responses to your questions, this oracle will deepen your kinship with the horse spirits so you can be enlivened by their freedom, grace, power, and agility — and feel these qualities reawaken in you, unbridled.

Kathy Pike is an energy healer and coach whose affinity with horses makes her a unique channel for their collective wisdom. The messages in this exquisitely illustrated set come direct from the horse spirits to show you who you are through their eyes and gently nudge you to find liberty in your strengths and confidence in your instincts.

Come home to your body, heart, and authenticity, forever changed by your encounters with *Oracle of the Sacred Horse*.

ISBN: 978-1-922573-72-8
41 cards and 144-page full-color guidebook set

Also available from Blue Angel Publishing®

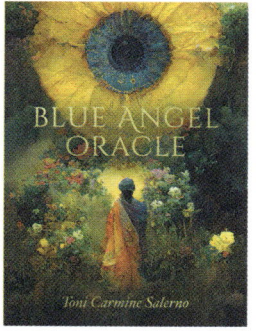

BLUE ANGEL ORACLE
New Earth Edition

TONI CARMINE SALERNO

Archangel Michael is here as your loving protector and guide. Journey with his presence to experience pathways of light and know the sacred space within your heart that connects you with eternal wisdom. This sublime oracle brings you to truth through the compassion and strength of the Blue Angel. The messages and imagery, both ethereal and familiar, embody and encourage the wonder of collaboration between you and the great unknowable creative intelligence of the Universe.

Answer your questions, doubts, challenges and curiosities with innovation, bliss and profound insight to go beyond all you currently see and dare to believe. Discover the immortal you and experience your world anew with *Blue Angel Oracle*.

ISBN: 978-1-922573-71-1
45 cards and 80-page full-color guidebook set

Also available from Blue Angel Publishing®

PRACTICAL MAGIC
An Oracle for Everyday Enchantment

SERENE CONNEELEY
Artwork by Selina Fenech

Energise the purpose, knowledge, and potential within you to empower your heart and transform your tomorrows. This inspired collaboration is a rich compendium of fascination, insight, ritual, symbolism, and divination that you can action in your daily life for surprising and satisfying results.

Journey into initiation and possibility, welcome adventure and reward, set nurturing boundaries, and shape your reality with the support of deities, herbs, crystals, color, the elements, and intention. Believe in your innate powers of creation and innovation, and charge your world with wonder — now and always.

ISBN: 978-1-922573-70-4
36 cards, 304-page guidebook and card stand set packaged in a deluxe hardcover box with magnetic close

Also available from Blue Angel Publishing®

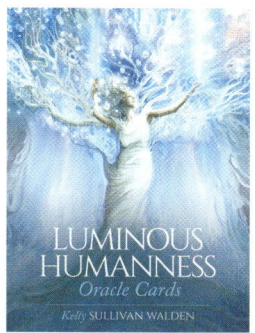

LUMINOUS HUMANNESS
ORACLE CARDS

KELLY SULLIVAN WALDEN
Artwork by Laila Savolainen

To be luminous is to be at ease with your inner gold. In feeling and freeing your authentic, connected, and whole self, your light illuminates your path and possibilities so you can move forward in confidence and clarity, excited for all that awaits you.

Bestselling author Kelly Sullivan Walden rolls insight, imagination, and joy into this gorgeous oracle, elevating perspective and turning everyday tedium into treasured moments and glowing experiences. Laila Savolainen's artworks allow you to hold the transcendent in your hands and its truths in your heart. Play with these cards for a few minutes each day to invite a more radiant life to meet you, wherever you are at.

ISBN: 978-1-922573-69-8
44 cards and 116-page guidebook set

Notes

Notes

For more information on this or any Blue Angel Publishing® release, visit our website:

www.blueangelonline.com